D1242493

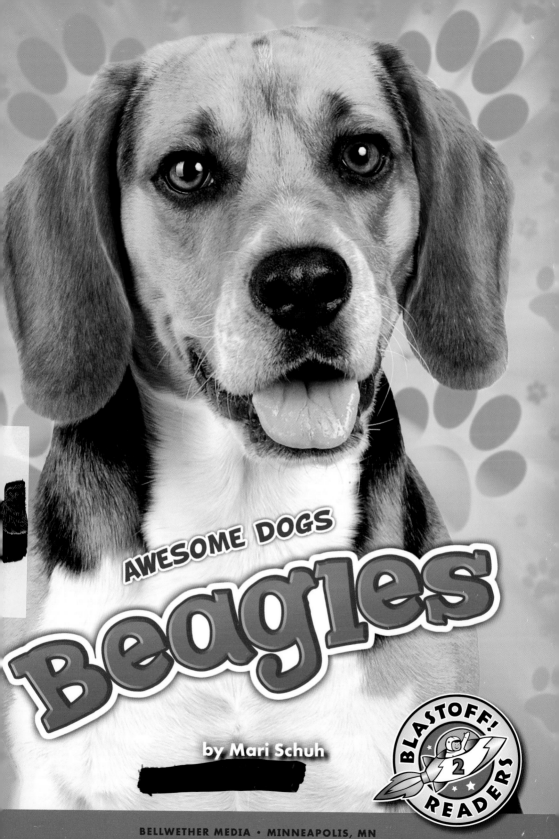

AWESOME DOGS

Beagles

by Mari Schuh

BELLWETHER MEDIA · MINNEAPOLIS, MN

Note to Librarians, Teachers, and Parents:

Blastoff! Readers are carefully developed by literacy experts and combine standards-based content with developmentally appropriate text.

Level 1 provides the most support through repetition of high-frequency words, light text, predictable sentence patterns, and strong visual support.

Level 2 offers early readers a bit more challenge through varied simple sentences, increased text load, and less repetition of high-frequency words.

Level 3 advances early-fluent readers toward fluency through increased text and concept load, less reliance on visuals, longer sentences, and more literary language.

Level 4 builds reading stamina by providing more text per page, increased use of punctuation, greater variation in sentence patterns, and increasingly challenging vocabulary.

Level 5 encourages children to move from "learning to read" to "reading to learn" by providing even more text, varied writing styles, and less familiar topics.

Whichever book is right for your reader, Blastoff! Readers are the perfect books to build confidence and encourage a love of reading that will last a lifetime!

This edition first published in 2016 by Bellwether Media, Inc.

No part of this publication may be reproduced in whole or in part without written permission of the publisher. For information regarding permission, write to Bellwether Media, Inc., Attention: Permissions Department, 5357 Penn Avenue South, Minneapolis, MN 55419.

Library of Congress Cataloging-in-Publication Data

Schuh, Mari C., 1975- author.
  Beagles / by Mari Schuh.
    pages cm. – (Blastoff! Readers. Awesome Dogs)
  Summary: "Relevant images match informative text in this introduction to beagles. Intended for students in kindergarten through third grade"– Provided by publisher.
  Audience: Ages 5-8
  Audience: K to grade 3
  Includes bibliographical references and index.
  ISBN 978-1-62617-237-1 (hardcover: alk. paper)
  1. Beagle (Dog breed)–Juvenile literature. I. Title.
  SF429.B3S38 2016
  636.753'7–dc23

                          2015007776

Printed in the United States of America, North Mankato, MN.

Table of Contents

Beagles are a small **breed** of dog. They are full of energy.

Their excellent sense of smell
makes them good hunters.

Short legs keep beagles close to the ground. It is easy to sniff for **scents**.

Their floppy ears trap the scents close to their noses.

7

Beagles have short, thick **coats**.

They are usually black, tan, and white.

These dogs come in two sizes. Small beagles are up to 13 inches (33 centimeters) tall.

Bigger beagles are 13 to 15 inches (33 to 38 centimeters) tall.

History of Beagles

No one knows the beagle's entire history.

England

N
W E
S

Today's beagles probably came from hunting dogs in England.

In the 1800s, small hunting dogs called beagles lived in the United States.

English beagles came to the
U.S. in the 1860s.

The two kinds of beagles were **bred** to create the beagles we know today.

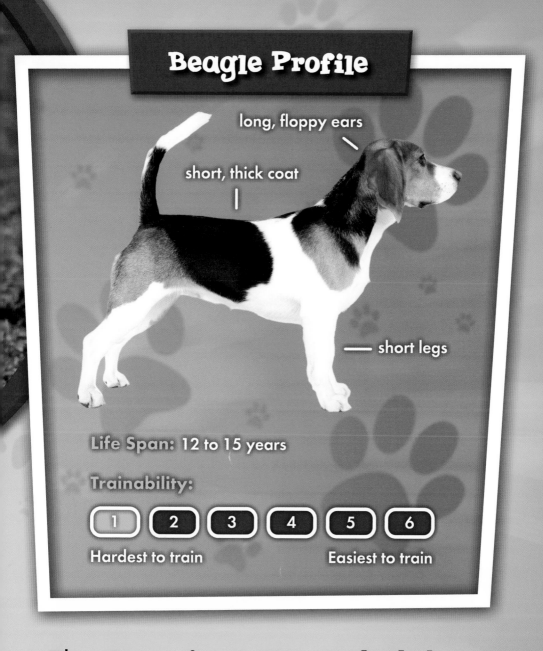

Beagle Profile

long, floppy ears

short, thick coat

short legs

Life Span: 12 to 15 years

Trainability:

1   2   3   4   5   6

Hardest to train   Easiest to train

The **American Kennel Club** puts the breed in the **Hound Group** for their hunting history.

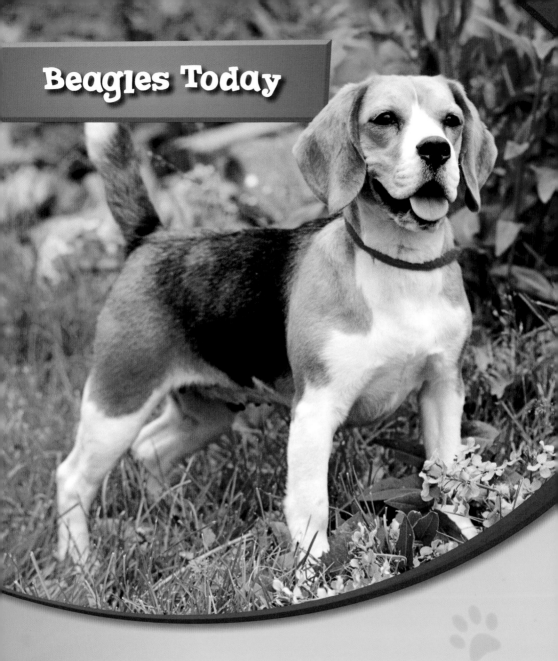

Beagles are noisy dogs. They bark to tell hunters they have found a scent.

They also bark to get their owners' attention. The dogs often **howl** when they are bored or sad.

Some beagles work. They sniff bags at airports to find illegal **foreign** plants and foods.

Beagles also enjoy being around people and other dogs. They are gentle and playful family pets!

Glossary

American Kennel Club—an organization that keeps track of dog breeds in the United States

bred—purposely mated two dogs to make puppies with certain qualities

breed—a type of dog

coats—the hair or fur covering some animals

foreign—from another country

Hound Group—a group of dog breeds that often have a history of hunting

howl—to make a long, loud, sad noise

scents—odors and smells

To Learn More

AT THE LIBRARY
Albright, Rosie. *Bedbug-sniffing Beagles and Other Scent Hounds.* New York, N.Y.: PowerKids Press, 2012.

Bozzo, Linda. *I Like Beagles!* Berkeley Heights, N.J.: Enslow Elementary, 2012.

Shores, Erika L. *All About Beagles.* North Mankato, Minn.: Capstone Press, 2013.

ON THE WEB
Learning more about beagles is as easy as 1, 2, 3.

1. Go to www.factsurfer.com.

2. Enter "beagles" into the search box.

3. Click the "Surf" button and you will see a list of related web sites.

With factsurfer.com, finding more information is just a click away.

Index

The images in this book are reproduced through the courtesy of: olaser, front cover; Jagodka, p. 4; Peter Kirillov, p. 5; Igor Normann, p. 6; Eric Isselee, pp. 7, 10 (left, right); Ann-Britt, p. 8; Minden Pictures/ SuperStock, p. 9; Faith A. Uridel/ KimballStock, p. 11; gbarinov, p. 12; Soloviova Liudmyla, pp. 13, 15; Farlap/ Alamy, p. 14; Goldika, p. 16; Vivienstock, p. 17; Mark Raycroft/ Minden Pictures/ Corbis, p. 18; Halfpoint, p. 19; Stephen J. Boitano/ AP Images, p. 20; Lunja, p. 21.